Let Your  ie

Written by: Ann King Lishinski

Illustrated by: Jaime Lishinski

Let Your Light Shine
by Ann King Lishinski

Illustrated by:
Jaime Lishinski

Editing and Layout by:
Charles Morello
IRIS Enterprises
Eveleth, MN 55734

Published by:

Singing River Publications
P.O. Box 72
Ely, MN 55731
www.speravi.com/singingriver

Printed by:
service printers of duluth, inc.
127 East Second Street
Duluth, Minnesota

ISBN: 0-9709575-0-5

1. Children's Stories; 2. Organ Donation; 3. Inspiration; 4. Friendship;
5. Stories in Rhyme

Acknowledgements

Thank you to:

Jaime-
> for the first spark, for all of your work during mid-terms, for your belief in me, your creativity and your love.

Gary-
> for your unending support and confidence. Thank you for being at my side through life's journey. Hold my hand while we keep walking.

Mom-
> for teaching me strength and courage. You are one of the strongest people I know. Remember "Onward Christian Soldier".

Frank, Ben, and Betsy-
> for listening, helping me find myself and teaching me more than you'll ever know.
> (P.S. You're not done yet.)

Lake Superior Magazine, Duluth, Minnesota

Andrew's Cameras, Virginia, Minnesota

Life Source, St. Paul, Minnesota

In memory
of Ms. Jessica Ann Lishinski

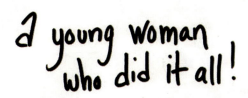

a young woman who did it all!

... forever in our hearts...

JL

I dedicate this book to the six recipients of my daughter's vital organs.
You are positives I cling to. You are lights in my life.

AKL

Preface

I have written this story as a tribute to my daughter, Jess. It carries a message that I know Jess would like to have told. It is a story about hard work, possibilities, kindness and sharing. It was an easy story to write. It flowed from thoughts of Jess. It is a book for children of all ages.

The title, *Let Your Light Shine*, was Jess' grandmother's line in a Sunday School program 75 years ago.

Jess died as the result of an accident. This is not revealed in my story, nor is this meant to be a sad book. It is a celebration of Jess' life.

I have included afterwords about Jess and about organ donation. If you are uncomfortable with the information, or if it is inappropriate for your child at this time, please fold the back jacket flap in at the end of the story.

Besides being a story of inspiration for youth, I want this book to send a positive message about organ donation. I would like to touch the hearts of loved ones of both donors and recipients, as we really are *one* family.

Jess' family and friends were dealt a terrible blow in the spring of 1999. To find something positive in the death of one's child is next to impossible – but I did find one thing. From the moment Jess' surgeon said the words "organ donor," I focused on the vision of families receiving phone calls saying, "We've found a heart for your mother" or, "We've found lungs for your daughter." Their situations were the antitheses of our reality. Jess was able to give one more time – and save or extend the lives of six individuals. For that, I am thankful.

I hope that you enjoy my story – as well as the illustrations drawn by my daughter, Jaime!

AKL

Preface for Younger Readers

Did you know that you can make the world a better, brighter place?

You have a light in your soul that you can turn on high or low. Never use the dimmer switch.

You can let your light shine by doing your best at everything, working your hardest, being kind and sharing.

You may not choose to shine in the same areas as the young girl in this story, but whatever you do — do your best and aim high.

There is a saying —
"With your life you can choose to shed light or cast a shadow."

Choose to shed light!

AKL

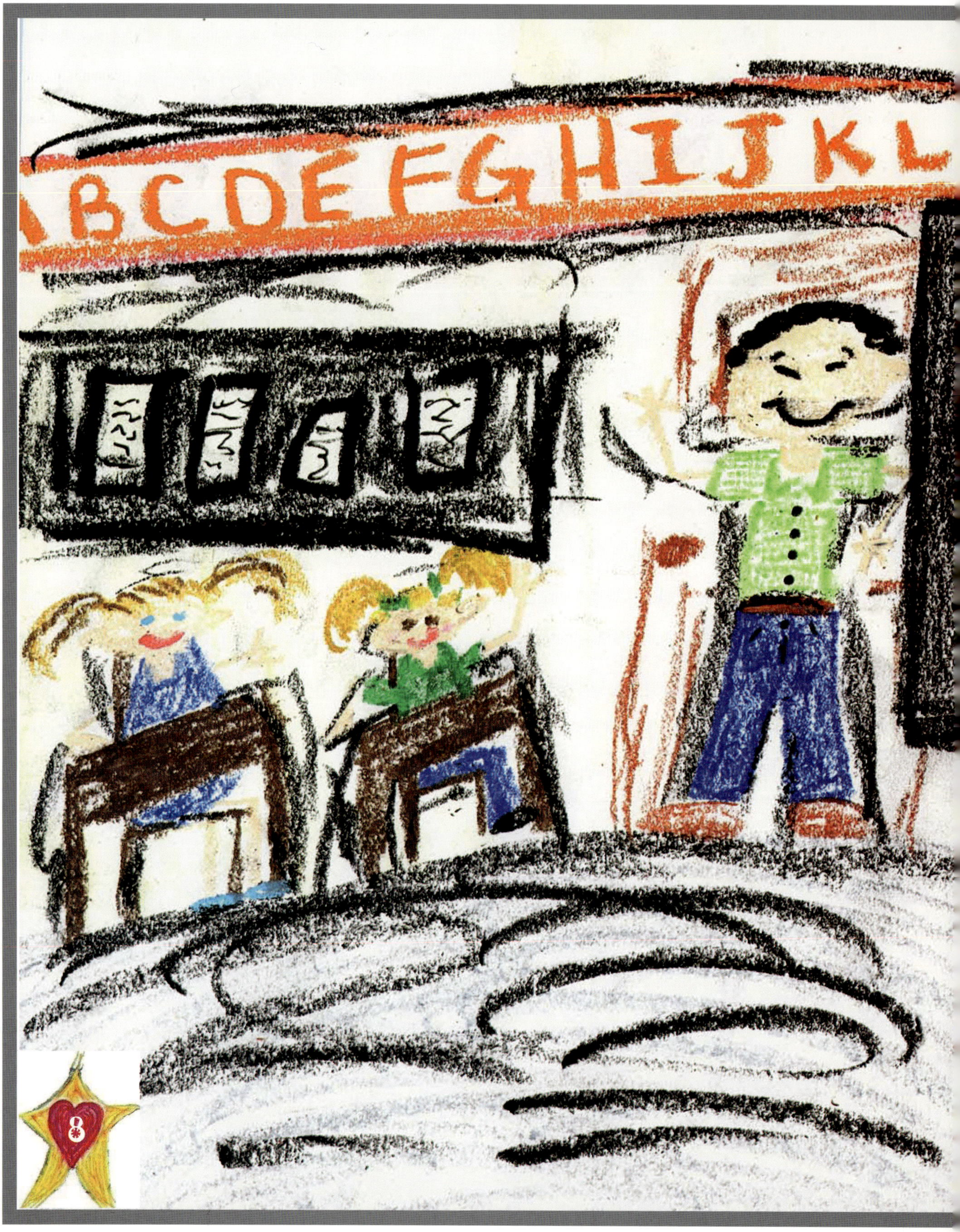
BCDEFGHIJKL

NOPQRSTUVWXYZ

You can be an awesome student.
Try hard and do your best.

You can ribbon in writing contests by doing better than the rest.

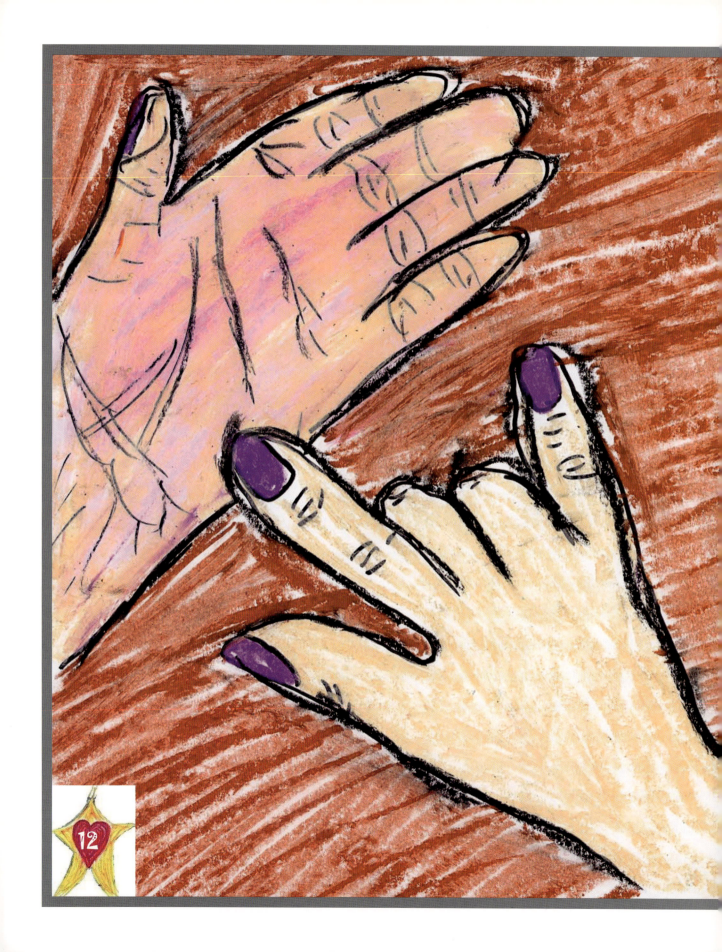

LOVE

You can learn to sign, communicate

and make

some

special

friends.

13

Lead service clubs around your town.

(There are needs that never end.)

Clean Up!

15

One day you could be president

of your marching band.

Even play a mean piano

by using just one hand.

Oops! That's my dog!

(or two!)

You could
captain
your high
school
ski team

and help them win a race.

21

Travel the world over
trying to find your
favorite
place.

Maybe a third world orphanage
is where you'll make your mark.

There are millions of kids
around the world
whose lives are in the dark.

25

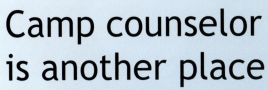

Camp counselor
is another place
    where you could learn to shine.

Be a friend to youth
    who need your smile
to make their day go fine.

28

Perhaps you'll be a pilot

sitting high up
on your perch.

Help other folks with kindness

Pastor Catfish

Teen Deacon

as an officer in your church.

31

Might you
serve
in your
state capitol

as a page when you're a teen?

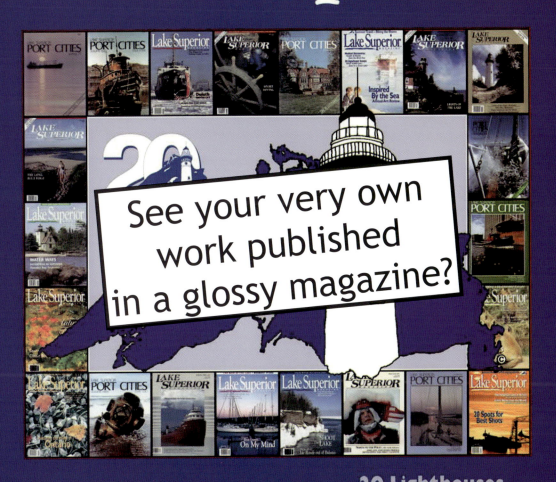

Anniversary Collector's Edition

Lake Superior
MAGAZINE ™

See your very own
work published
in a glossy magazine?

September 1999
$3.95   Canada $4.95

0 74470 19015 8

www.lakesuperior.com

20 Lighthouses
Fall Travel Planner
20 Years of Favorites
Readers' "Best of the Lake"

35

Be voted by your classmates as "Most Likely to Succeed"?

(It will help if you remember through your childhood to read!)

You could touch a lot of people's lives.

You have many gifts to share.

Just keep in mind that if you try

you can go

ANYWHERE!

How do I know all this?" you ask.
I guess I'll now confess.

The girl
this story
is all
about

goes by
the
name of
'Jess'.

Now, *Let Your Light Shine* every day.

Today's the day to start.

Do your very best in everything

and always share your heart!

43

This is a picture Jess drew of her family when she was five years old.

About Jess

Jess is an incredible spirit who graced us with her presence for twenty-one years. From a young age she believed that just about anything was possible. Jess never gave up. She set goals and worked hard to achieve them. She was an avid reader, talented writer, skier, kayaker and pilot. She loved Lake Superior. Each possibility in this story was accomplished by Jess. She has proud parents and siblings.

At the time of Jess' death she was a senior at St. Cloud State University in Minnesota, where she was studying journalism and aviation.

Jess died as the result of an in-line skating accident in 1999. Several years earlier, she made it known in conversation at home, that should she ever be in the unfortunate position, she would want to be an organ donor.

AKL

Organ Donation Information

- There is no cost to donor families for donation.

- Organs that can be donated are the heart, lungs, liver, kidneys, pancreas and small intestines. One organ donor can save the lives of eight people.

- Approximately 80,000 Americans are waiting to receive lifesaving organ transplants. A new name is added to the national waiting list every 16 minutes. Unfortunately, 16 people die each day waiting for an organ.

- There are more than 20,000 organ transplants performed in the U.S. annually. Transplants have become a successful form of treatment for end-stage organ disease. Three-year patient success rates are estimated at 95% for kidney transplants, 92% for pancreas transplants, 91% for heart transplants, 90% for liver transplants, 81% for heart-lung transplants, and 76% for lung transplants.

- Families often find that donation helps them through their grieving process. They receive great personal benefit by being able to have something positive come from the death of a loved one. For recipients, organ transplants offer a second chance at life.

- You can become an organ donor by indicating "yes" on your driver's license or ID card and telling your family your wishes.

For more information on Organ Donation, please contact:

Life Source
2550 University Avenue
Suite 315
St. Paul, MN 55114

About the Author

Ann King Lishinski wrote this story about her daughter, Jess. Ann lives on Minnesota's Iron Range and summers in Eagle Harbor, Michigan. She is a graduate of Suomi College (now Finlandia University) and Michigan Technological University. Ann resides with her husband, Gary; son, Matt; and 100-pound baby, Tag (the pianist in this story). This is her first book.

About the Illustrator

Jaime Lishinski is the daughter of the author of this book. She is completing a degree in elementary education at St. Cloud State University, St. Cloud, Minnesota. Jaime loves hockey, children, hockey, dogs, hockey, Monday night chicken, hockey, and driving her truck. This is also her first book.